THE BARS AⱤ
OF YORK

A Handbook for Visitors

by R. M. Butler M.A., Ph.D., F.S.A.

Former Investigator, Royal Commission on Historical
    Monuments (England)
Hon. Editor, The Yorkshire Archaeological
    Journal

The heart of York is surrounded by the finest remaining circuit of medieval walls in England. They were built during the thirteenth and fourteenth centuries and stand for most of their length of just over 2 miles on a massive earth rampart thrown up in the ninth to eleventh centuries and in places concealing Roman walls. The four major gates, or Bars, and thirty-seven interval towers still remain, although four of the six posterns and nine other towers have been rebuilt or destroyed. In this handbook the history of the defences is briefly surveyed after the principal points of interest to be seen in a walk round the walls have been described, starting at Bootham Bar and proceeding clockwise around the City.

A map of the defences appears on pages 18 and 19.

Bootham Bar in about 1820

2

A WALK ROUND THE WALLS

For the purpose of this handbook the circuit is described commencing at Bootham Bar, but the wall-walk can be reached at several points as well as at the four main Bars — at Layerthorpe Bridge, the Red Tower, Fishergate Bar, Fishergate Postern, below Baile Hill, at Victoria Bar, Station Road, and North Street Postern. The walls are built almost entirely of magnesian limestone quarried near Tadcaster, although some gritstone blocks may be observed, apparently robbed from ruined Roman buildings. The curtain wall is generally about 6 ft. wide (1.8 m.) and 13 ft. high (4 m.), including the embattled parapet of 6 ft. high. The outer ditch, once 60 ft. wide (18.3 m.) and 10 ft. deep (3 m.) but only water-filled around the Walmgate sector, has been filled in nearly every-where. The impressive rampart, at its best 100 ft. wide (30 m.) and 30 ft. high (9 m.), still supports the stone walls and incorporates not only the smaller ramparts thrown up by the Danes and Normans but from Bootham Bar to Monk Bar also conceals the Roman fortress wall and its rampart. The length of the wall-walk is just under 2 miles (3.2 km.), but the intervening stretches of water once brought the perimeter to 2 miles 5 furlongs (4.2 km.).

FROM BOOTHAM BAR TO MONK BAR

Bootham Bar stands on the site of the main north-west gateway of the Roman legionary fortress of Eburacum but has only one archway against three in the Roman gateway. (The present side archways are 19th cent-ury). Its outer archway is some of the oldest masonry visible along the circuit, since it was built soon after the Norman Conquest when the Bar was still known as Galmanlith. The two-storeyed gatehouse above the passageway has been much altered since it was first erected in the four-teenth century. The bartizans or hanging turrets on the outer side and the upper floor were probably rebuilt after the siege of 1644 following damage from bombardment. The barbican or outer defence, which this like all the four main Bars possessed, was finally demolished in 1835; it resembled the one still standing at Walmgate Bar. The inner half of the gatehouse is of 1835 and replaced a classical facade of 1719 with a central niche housing a statue of Ebrauk, the legendary pre-Roman founder of York. This facade had itself replaced a three-gabled half-timbered house, probably built in 1583.

The statues on top of the Bar were carved in 1894 to replace the crumbling remains of older figures. They are by George Milburn and represent a fourteenth-century mayor flanked by a mason and a knight. The coats of arms below, renewed in 1969, show the Stuart royal arms and on the smaller shields the city arms. The remains of the portcullis, a heavy wooden grille with spiked bottom sliding in vertical grooves, are now fixed in place and can be seen within the passageway and from the first floor, reached now by a Victorian stairway placed inappropriately against the outer face of the walls. It should be noted that there are no doorways to the barbican parapet walk from the first floor as at the other Bars, indicating that here the barbican was an afterthought not envisaged in the original design of the gateway.

Although it was the main entrance to the City from the north-west, Bootham Bar has fewer notable historical associations than the other gateways. The severed head of Thomas Mowbray was fixed here in 1405. The Bar was unsuccessfully attacked in 1487 by the Lords Scrope on behalf of Lambert Simnell. It was bombarded in 1644 by the Earl of Manchester's troops and was restored in 1651. An additional archway for pedestrians was made in 1771. The whole Bar was nearly demolished to make way for St. Leonard's Place in 1831, but was eventually restored in 1835. It again needed restoration in 1951 and was underpinned, strengthened and cleaned in 1969.

The walls follow the line of the Roman fortress defences. It has only been possible to enjoy the walk along their summit with its fine views of the Minster and Dean's Park since the restoration of 1887-9, when the arches supporting the wall-walk were added. The outer faces of the wall and rampart up to the north angle have long been concealed by the houses of Gillygate (named from St. Giles' Church which stood near the present Salvation Army Citadel). Houses had been built along the edge of the outer ditch here as early as 1170, and although the Royalists set fire to them in 1644 in case they provided cover for an attack they were rebuilt after the Civil War and still (1974) hide four of the five towers along this stretch. Three of these towers are demi-hexagonal and were probably added in the late fourteenth or fifteenth century. The second tower from the Bar has a circular gunport of about 1440 near its base. All the towers have battlements of 1887-9, and the large round one at the angle was added at that time. The tower which had stood here, called at various times Bawing, Frost Tower, and Robin Hood Tower, had disappeared by 1680, and its modern successor with its small merlons and two rows of arrow-slits was built on the advice of G. T. Clark, a leading expert on medieval military architecture.

Lord Mayor's Walk, first called by that name in about 1700, but probably originally a street in the twelfth-century suburb of Newbiggin, runs along the outer edge of the ditch, here preserved in a condition most like its original form. The tower next to the angle has little turrets, quite impractical for archers to use, and a shield, all added in 1887, but its base is original. A bronze plaque on the inside of the parapet records

4

the end of a dispute when Edwin Gray claimed to own part of the wall and rampart. Nearer Monk Bar two depressions can be seen in the rampart, one marking the site of a destroyed tower, and the other indicating the position of the Roman north-east gate and its Norman successor. The lines of the Roman streets approaching it are preserved inside the walls by Chapter House Street and outside by Groves Lane, now only a narrow alley, running towards Monk Bridge over the Foss. From this stretch of the wall-walk there are good views of the twelfth-century chapel in which is kept the Minster Library and which is almost the last relic of the medieval Archbishop's Palace, and of the seventeenth-century Treasurer's House with its rear wings, now called Gray's Court, which incorporates parts of a Norman building.

Monk Bar probably replaced an earlier entrance on the Roman site to the north-west in about 1330, a change made because the cathedral

Monk Bar   Crown Copyright

5

clergy objected to a main road running through their Close, and because Goodramgate had replaced the Roman street as a route towards the exit to Malton and Scarborough. The Bar, at first called Monkgate Bar, is the loftiest (63 ft. high, 19.2 m.) and strongest of the medieval gateways. It was built as a self-contained fortress with every floor defensible even if others were captured. The lower three storeys are vaulted in stone, and so are fireproof, and the stairways leading to each floor in the thickness of a side wall are so placed that an enemy must cross a room to reach the next stair.

Features to note on the outer facade are the doorways to the barbican and the gallery supported on an arch from which missiles could be dropped through holes, now blocked, on attackers who had broken through the outer gates. The coats of arms, each below decorated canopies, are the Plantagenet royal arms (before nineteenth - century restoration they bore the many fleurs-de-lys of Edward III or Richard II) and the arms of the city of York. The uppermost storey was added in the fifteenth century and the two square gun-ports with cruciform sighting slits above the gallery belong to that date. The turrets were heightened at the same time, but the six figures of wild men grasping boulders are probably seventeenth-century replacements of earlier carvings.

Portcullis Windlass   Crown Copyright

This Bar is the only one to have a medieval stone inner facade; the others were probably built with open backs, later filled with timber-framed walls. The purpose of the narrow open gallery is unknown, and nothing has stood in the three niches since artists first started sketching the Bar. The narrow opening in the wall thickness leading to the first floor is now also used for access to the wall-walk. A blocked archway in one side of the main passageway once led to a guardhouse beside the Bar. The portcullis is still in working order and the ancient windlass with iron ratchet and paul remains on the second floor. On either side of it are doors to the tiny circular rooms in the turrets: one of these rooms was probably the Little Ease where recusant Catholics and mutinous apprentices were confined during the sixteenth century when the Bar became a prison for York Freemen who broke the law. The barbican, peculiar in having polygonal turrets and a sallyport in one side, used in 1644 by the Royalist cavalry, was demolished in 1826. The side arches were added then and the larger one was widened for vehicles in 1861.

FROM MONK BAR TO JEWBURY

The wall-walk is reached by modern stairs beside the Bar and is supported on arches, some of which already existed in 1634 and were probably added in the reign of Henry VII. Inside the walls a length of Roman fortress wall with an interval tower and the east angle tower has been uncovered. At the angle, the Roman wall stands to a height of 16 ft. (4.8 m.), including the cornice below the battlements which would have brought the height to 24 ft. (7.3 m.). This portion dates from the restoration carried out under the emperor Septimius Severus in about 200. The destroyed south-east wall of the fortress ran from this corner to a multangular tower under the modern Feasegate by way of the south-east gate sited where King's Square now is. This gate was perhaps made into a stronghold by the Danish Kings of York and destroyed by King Athelstan in 927 but still recalled by the modern name.

A ruined brick ice-house of about 1800 is dug into the outer face of the ramparts near Monk Bar and a broad buttress near the first tower has two arched openings visible from the wall-walk — lavatories for the guards or for a house built later on top of the walls. The first tower, called in 1380 'the tower opposite Harlot Hill near Petrehall', has nineteenth-century turrets but a medieval base and arrow-slits. There may have been a postern gate near here leading to Love Lane, which runs outside the defences continuing the line of St. Andrewgate within the walls. It would have been N.W. of the Merchant Taylors' Guildhall, still to be seen from the parapet walk. At the next tower the rampart and wall make a curve to the south-east and then turn abruptly to east-north-east. This is apparently because the first length is part of the defences of the Danish city, curving towards a flood bank and landing stages on the banks of the Foss (found in excavations when the Telephone Exchange in Hungate was built), and the second is a Norman extension to include St. Cuthbert's Church and the low-lying Peasholme. The oval tower in the angle, called 'new' in 1380, has a nineteenth-century parapet above the ancient base. Blocked embrasures in the walls to the east are a clue to a period when the wall was lower; the small buttressess near them are also of an early type. Outside the walls traces of the ditch remain, and the street named Jewbury recalls land belonging to the jewish community expelled in 1290, perhaps their cemetery.

FROM JEWBURY TO THE RED TOWER

The rampart diminishes in size as the defences approach the river Foss. Two towers here are closely spaced. The first is rectangular with a massive stepped base and musket-loops in the parapet wall. The second, where the wall now ends, is unlike any other, since it is partly supported on an arch and partly on corbels. This curious support may be due either to the marshy position or to hasty restoration after the Civil War, but it has certainly looked like this since 1700. From this tower the wall originally continued for a further 70 ft. (21.3 m.) to Layerthorpe Postern at the head of the bridge over the Foss, demolished when the bridge was rebuilt in 1829. The appearance of this postern, a rectangular tower with an arched passage and a gabled roof, is well known from many drawings. It was probably built in the fourteenth century, and was heightened in 1604 to form a house over the passage.

The next stretch of the city walls is 450 yds. (410 m.) from Layerthorpe Bridge, on the other side of the river beside Foss Islands Road and now some distance from the water's edge. This name recalls the fact that until 1850 marshy islands amid shallow streams still gave some indication of the extent of the King's Fishpool. Fishing rights and the use of boats on the pool were strictly controlled by medieval kings, who appointed its Keepers, but from the seventeenth-century drainage, encroachment, and the growth of reed beds gradually reduced the extent of the water. The canalisation of the river as far as Sheriff Hutton Bridge in 1792 as the Foss Navigation, gave the stream a deeper and straighter course, hastening the drying up of the pool.

The Red Tower was built in 1490 as part of the strengthening of York's defences ordered by Henry VII. The work had been entrusted to the bricklayers or tilers, and the stonemasons resenting this, smashed their tools and threatened to maim or kill them. Consequently, when a tiler called John Patrick was found murdered in 1491 the wardens of the masons' guild were committed for trial. They were, however, never convicted. The tower's name refers to the colour of the bricks and it was often described as standing 'in the water of Foss'. Its appearance has changed greatly since then, for not only have some 5 ft. (1.5 m.) of the base, including massive limestone footings, been buried, but the original flat leaded roof with embattled parapet has been replaced by a tiled hipped roof and most of the windows, like this roof, date from the restoration of 1858. As at Monk Bar, Walmgate Bar and the contemporary Fishergate Postern Tower, there is a projecting lavatory supported on corbels. The tower which had been in ruins from as early as 1735, became known as the Brimstone House. It was patched up in about 1800 with a gabled roof for use as a stable.

FROM THE RED TOWER TO FISHERGATE POSTERN

From the Red Tower to Walmgate Bar the wall is low, as is the rampart on which it stands, and has been much restored. It was probably built in the mid-fourteenth century, and features going back to that date are the two solid rectangular towers and the foundation arches intended to relieve the weight of the masonry on the unstable bank and still visible in places. The internal arches supporting the wall-walk are probably work of about 1500, but the original date of the small cruciform arrow-slits below canopies which appear in several merlons is unknown. In their present form they are largely nineteenth-century work, but some such slits already existed before this restoration.

Walmgate Bar incorporates a twelfth-century archway and so existed as a stone gateway through earth ramparts crowned with a palisade for nearly two hundred years before the adjoining city walls were erected. It retains its barbican, similar to those which formerly existed at the other three main Bars, as well as its portcullis and fifteenth-century inner wooden gates. It has suffered more damage and has consequently been more restored than the other gateways, for it was burned in 1489 by rebels under John Chambers and was battered during the siege of 1644 by the cannon on Lamel Hill and in St. Laurence's Churchyard. A mine dug under the gateway at this time was revealed by a captured Parliamentary soldier before it could be exploded, but the sag visible in the side walls of the barbican is probably due to it. It seems that the whole upper storey on the outer side as well as much of the barbican had to be rebuilt after the siege, completion in 1648 being marked by an inscription over the outermost arch. Restoration was again needed in 1840, to which date belong most of the barbican parapet and the smaller side archway. A tablet recording this restoration can be seen below the medieval royal arms over the main outer arch. The larger side arch is of 1862.

The inner facade of the Bar is of great interest, for it is a timber-framed and plastered house in the classical style of the late sixteenth century. It still preserves its Roman Doric and Ionic columns and mullioned windows, although embellishments recorded in the Chamberlains' Accounts of 1584-6 — such features as royal arms and lions in wood or plaster and iron wind vanes — have long since vanished. The house was the birthplace in 1793 of John Browne, the artist and historian of York Minster.

From Walmgate Bar to Fishergate Bar: there are few features of interest in this stretch of the walls.

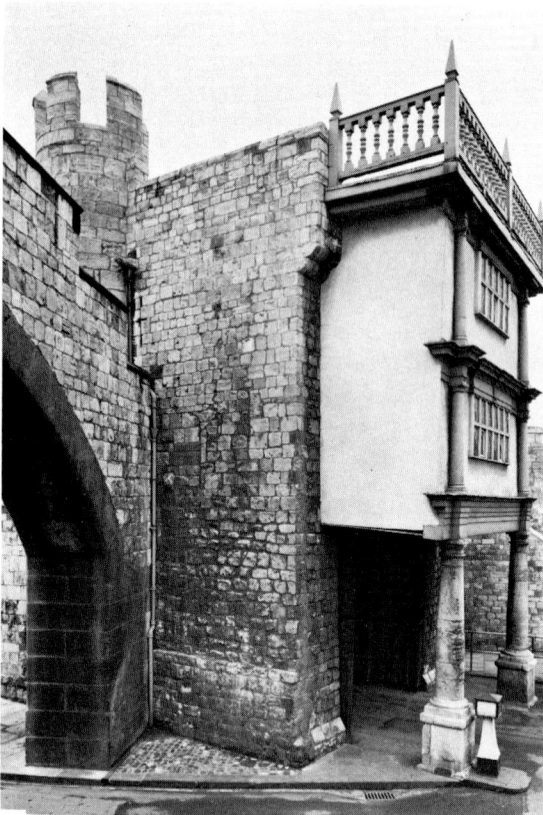

Elizabethan House, Walmgate Bar

The rampart was cut back, on the outside in 1827 for the pens of the Cattle Market, recently moved to Murton, on the inside in 1830 for the back yards of small houses, since demolished. Its external slope has now been restored. Many of the embrasures of the parapet have been narrowed to form musket-loops. There remains only one small rectangular tower between the two gateways. The chamfered plinth which can be seen intermittently along the base of the curtain wall resembles that to the west of Fishergate Bar, which can be ascribed to 1345.

Fishergate Bar is one of the most puzzling features of the defences. A gate existed here in the mid-fourteenth century, but the present gateway with its wide central arch, grooved for a portcullis, and two flanking

10

passageways appears to be fifteenth-century work. There is apparently a reference to one of these side passages in 1422, and new wooden gates were made for the Bar in 1442, when a quantity of stone was also used for building here. Two inscriptions were set up near this point in 1487 by the Lord Mayor, Sir William Todd, to record the construction at his own expense of 60 yds. (55 m.) of wall. One of these, with similar wording and city arms on both sides, is now set above the main arch; the other, with two damaged figures and shields with Todd's personal mark below a canopy, is in the Yorkshire Museum. In May 1489, however, rebels damaged this gateway so badly that it was bricked up and remained blocked until re-opened . in 1827. Marks of fire from this attack can be seen on the jambs of the central arch. The blocked gateway, which then had two towers rising above the wall, was used under Elizabeth I and her successor as a prison for Roman Catholics and lunatics. In the late seventeenth century some of the masonry, no doubt from the upper part, was used to repair the King's Staith and Castle Mills Bridge. The Bar has looked much as it does now since its restoration in 1827, but it is unknown whether it was originally provided with a barbican.

From Fishergate Bar to Fishergate Postern the wall and rampart, beyond another small tower,

Fishergate Postern Tower   Crown Copyright

11

bend southward, presumably to protect the end of the dam across the Foss. The rectangular tower on the tip of this salient has two cruciform gun-slits, probably inserted in about 1500, but the fireplace and brick vaults inside the tower were made soon after the Civil War. This tower and the adjoining wall have a continuous plinth and were built in 1345. Many masons' marks are visible in the outer facing of the curtain wall on the side towards the postern, perhaps due to the re-use of stone.

Fishergate Postern is a narrow pointed archway with provision for a portcullis. It is apparently fourteenth-century work, taken down and reset when the adjoining tower was built. This postern was described in the Middle Ages as 'near Scarlet Pit' or 'near St. George's Church'.

Fishergate Postern Tower was built in about 1505 to replace an earlier structure called Talkan Tower after Robert de Talkan, Mayor in 1399. It was called Edward's Tower in the seventeenth century, but the reason for this name is unknown. The tower is well-built of smoothly dressed and carefully jointed masonry, but surprisingly has few military features other than its height of three storeys. A spiral staircase is contained in a little turret on the south side which originally rose above a flat roof with crenellated parapets but is now hidden under a tiled hipped roof supported on sixteenth or seventeenth-century beams. Windows have been formed in the original embrasures of the parapet. There is a projecting garderobe (latrine) on the first floor.

YORK CASTLE

York Castle lies across the Foss from this tower and still retains its thirteenth-century keep, Clifford's Tower, standing on the high mound originally raised by orders of William the Conqueror. This keep and the walls of Henry III's castle were probably designed by Henry de Reyns, the architect of the eastern arm of Westminster Abbey. Only two of the towers of the bailey wall remain and only footings and the drawbridge pit indicate the site of the great south gateway. The medieval halls where assizes were held and the towers where prisoners were confined have been replaced by three impressive eighteenth-century buildings. The Debtors' Prison of 1701-5 was perhaps designed by William Wakefield, while John Carr of York was responsible for the main outlines of the Assize Courts of 1773-7 and of the matching Female Prison of 1780 opposite it. The latter building has recently been linked to the Debtors' Prison by an entrance hall, and together they house the attractive Castle Museum. The Castle was much altered under George IV, when a new gatehouse, outer wall and prison blocks radiating from a governor's house were erected, but nearly every trace of these was removed in 1936.

Clifford's Tower, built by Henry III from 1245 to 1260 as a self-contained stronghold and royal residence, housed the Treasury during the

Scottish Wars of the fourteenth century, while the Courts of King's Bench and Common Pleas sat in the Castle halls. Although partly dismantled for his own profit by the avaricious gaoler, Robert Redhead, in 1592, it was restored in 1643 to hold a garrison by the last Earl of Cumberland, Henry Clifford, whose arms, together with those of Charles I, appear over the entrance. It remained a royal fortress until 1690, but on 23rd April 1684 lost its roof and floors in a disastrous fire and explosion. Throughout the eighteenth-century it was a picturesque ruin in a private garden, but in 1825 was enclosed within the prison walls, and later passed into the care of the Office of Works and was restored.

YORK CASTLE TO BAILE HILL

Castlegate Postern, a narrow archway with a portcullis flanked by a strong D-shaped tower, stood just beyond the wet moat which for centuries surrounded the base of the mound of Clifford's Tower. This postern was enlarged for carriages in 1699, but was demolished in 1826. The short stretch of wall beyond it, which still survives, was always low, but the raising of St. George's Field outside it to avoid flooding has made it appear even more insignificant. Blocked embrasures are visible in the wall and on the inside the narrow ledge below the parapet retains its medieval proportions — too narrow for patrolling but intended to support a temporary walk of planks in time of war.

Davy Tower, named after a medieval tenant, stands at the end of the city walls on the bank of the Ouse. It was also called Friars Minor Tower, from the important Franciscan Friary, once the lodging of kings, which lay between this length of wall and Lower Friargate. Part of the Friary boundary wall along the riverside, built in about 1290, still stands beside the esplanade. The appearance of the tower has been changed by the erection on top of it in about 1750 of a brick summer house. The postern between it and the river, built in 1732 to lead to the New Walk and replacing a seventeenth-century wooden public lavatory known as the Sugar House, was demolished in the last century. A chain, sold as redundant in 1553, could be stretched from Davy Tower across the Ouse to the corresponding tower on the opposite bank. This was the Crane Tower, a round tower resembling that still surviving at North Street Postern, and named from the Common Crane on a quay beside it.

Skeldergate Postern, an archway flanked by two turrets, was demolished in 1807-8, an act which provoked a lawsuit between the Archbishop and the Corporation, won by the former and so effectively deterring the city authorities from pulling down the rest of the walls, as the council had resolved to do. The length of wall from Skeldergate to the foot of Baile Hill, including a new archway made during the restoration of 1831, was cleared away in 1878 to provide access to the new Skeldergate Bridge. The wall-walk is now reached through a polygonal tower of that date.

BAILE HILL TO NORTH STREET POSTERN

Baile Hill is the principal remaining feature of the castle of the Old Baile, built by William the Conqueror to dominate the part of York south-west of the Ouse and, together with his other castle on the opposite bank, to control navigation. It soon became disused as a fortress, passed by 1200 into the hands of the Archbishops and then, in about 1460, to the city's possession. The bailey, a rectangular space surrounded by a ditch and earth rampart, lay to the north-west of the mound. Its gateway was attacked by citizens in 1308 and they were consequently excommunicated by the Archbishop. Later it was used for grazing cattle, for musters of armed citizens, for archery practice, and for traditional Shrove Tuesday games. The City and Ainsty Gaol was built here in 1802-7 but demolished in 1880, when houses were erected on the site of the bailey. Baile Hill is an artificial mound containing much Roman occupation material and stands on the site of a Roman cemetery outside the *colonia* wall. Excavations in 1968-9 have found evidence for a wooden tower on top of the mound approached by steep steps up the south-east face. Depressions in the rampart still mark the position of the ditch which surrounded the mound and cut it off from the castle bailey. During the Civil War two cannon were mounted on top of the hill, but in 1722 trees were first planted on its summit. For long the bailey was defended by a wooden palisade, but after the adjoining city wall was built the citizens persuaded the Archbishop to replace the palisade in stone, for it would otherwise have been a weak point in their defences.

The ditch, rampart and wall run in a straight line from the south angle tower in the Old Baile to the west angle of the defences; at the north end the rampart probably covers the Roman *colonia* wall, and the Danish defences succeeding it. Towers of three types — rounded, rectangular, and polygonal — can be seen along this stretch, the first shape being the earliest. The rounded south angle tower is probably the Bitch-daughter Tower mentioned in 1451 and 1566, when stones from it were used to repair Ouse Bridge. Its present brick-vaulted inner room with a fireplace was made in 1645, when a guardhouse and gun platform were built here.

Victoria Bar was pierced through the defences in 1838, as the inscription over the central arch relates (the side arches are later). When it was being made the workmen discovered a blocked ancient arch, the

Lounlith or hidden gate of medieval records. The semi-circular tower just beyond the Bar is probably that called Sadler Tower in 1380, and

Sadler Tower   Crown Copyright

has good internal embrasures to its arrow-slits and a battered base of mid-thirteenth century type. The next tower but one is similar but has remains of vaulting inside, probably once supporting an upper stage rising above the battlements. On the base of the next tower a head and crossed spades are carved to commemorate the laying out of a garden by the sculptor Mark Hessay. Nunnery Lane, named from the Bar Convent founded in 1686, skirts the outer edge of the ditch, which has been encroached upon by buildings and a car park.

Micklegate Bar, formerly called Micklelith or the great gate, incorporates a twelfth-century gritstone outer arch, and the walls of the passage are built of re-used Roman stonework, including coffins. The gatehouse above has lofty turrets with figures of knights (replacements of 1950) and its facade bears the royal arms of Edward III under a helm with lion crest, two shields of the city arms and, lower down, the arms of the Lord Mayor Sir John Lister-Kaye, commemorating a repair in 1737 (not 1727 as the inscription states). The doorways to the demolished barbican are visible. The rear of the Bar is work of 1827, replacing a timber-framed structure like that at Walmgate Bar, probably built in 1585. A side arch for pedestrians was made as early as 1753, but the present flanking archways are nineteenth-century. Parts of the portcullis are preserved inside the Bar, which was last substantially restored in 1954.

15

Because it was the most frequented city gate the severed heads or quarters of traitors and rebels were exhibited here in preference to the other Bars and the Castle gates, although those were also used. The heads of Sir Henry Percy (Hotspur) in 1403, of Richard, Duke of York in 1460, of Lancastrian leaders captured at Towton in 1461, of the Earl of Northumberland in 1572, of Puritan conspirators in 1663, and of Jacobites in 1746—all these and many others were stuck on poles above the Bar. The last of these sinister relics was not removed until 1754, stolen by a Jacobite tailor to the great indignation of the Government.

Micklegate Bar   Crown Copyright

The chief interest of Micklegate Bar is that, as the main entrance to the city from London, it was the usual place for ceremonial receptions of royal and distinguished visitors. Details are known of the pageantry arranged for the visits of Edward IV, Richard III, Henry VII, Margaret Tudor, Lord Burleigh, James I, Charles I on three occasions, and James II when Duke of York. Henry VIII was expected to come through this gateway and it was decked with his arms and those of Catherine Howard and Prince Edward, but in fact he entered by Walmgate Bar. The present Queen was welcomed here in June 1971.

From Micklegate Bar to North Street Postern. There is only a short length of wall with one plain rectangular tower and many external buttresses between the Bar and the west angle. The tower at this angle is mainly built of large gritstone blocks, unlike the limestone facing of

Near Micklegate Bar   Crown Copyright

other towers, but internally has a windowless brick-vaulted room. It was probably damaged during the siege of 1644 and rebuilt on the old pattern to support cannon. Its name, Tofts Tower, was derived from the King's Tofts within the walls, perhaps an early centre of county administration, an open space on the site of large Roman baths, where an ancient royal chapel was granted to the Dominican Friars in 1228. In the remainder, Toft Green, the carts and displays used in the annual Corpus Christi mystery plays were stored and so it was also called Pageant Green. A prison was built there in 1814, replaced in 1839 by the old railway station, now offices.

The north-west side of the defences has been affected by the piercing of arches, first for railway lines in 1839 and 1845, and then, when the present station was built, for access roads to it made in 1876. A small burial ground for victims of the cholera epidemic was consecrated in part of the outer ditch in 1832 and in 1860 the approaches to the new Lendal Bridge dwarfed the two towers beside the river. In spite of these changes the ramparts still remain impressive along this stretch,

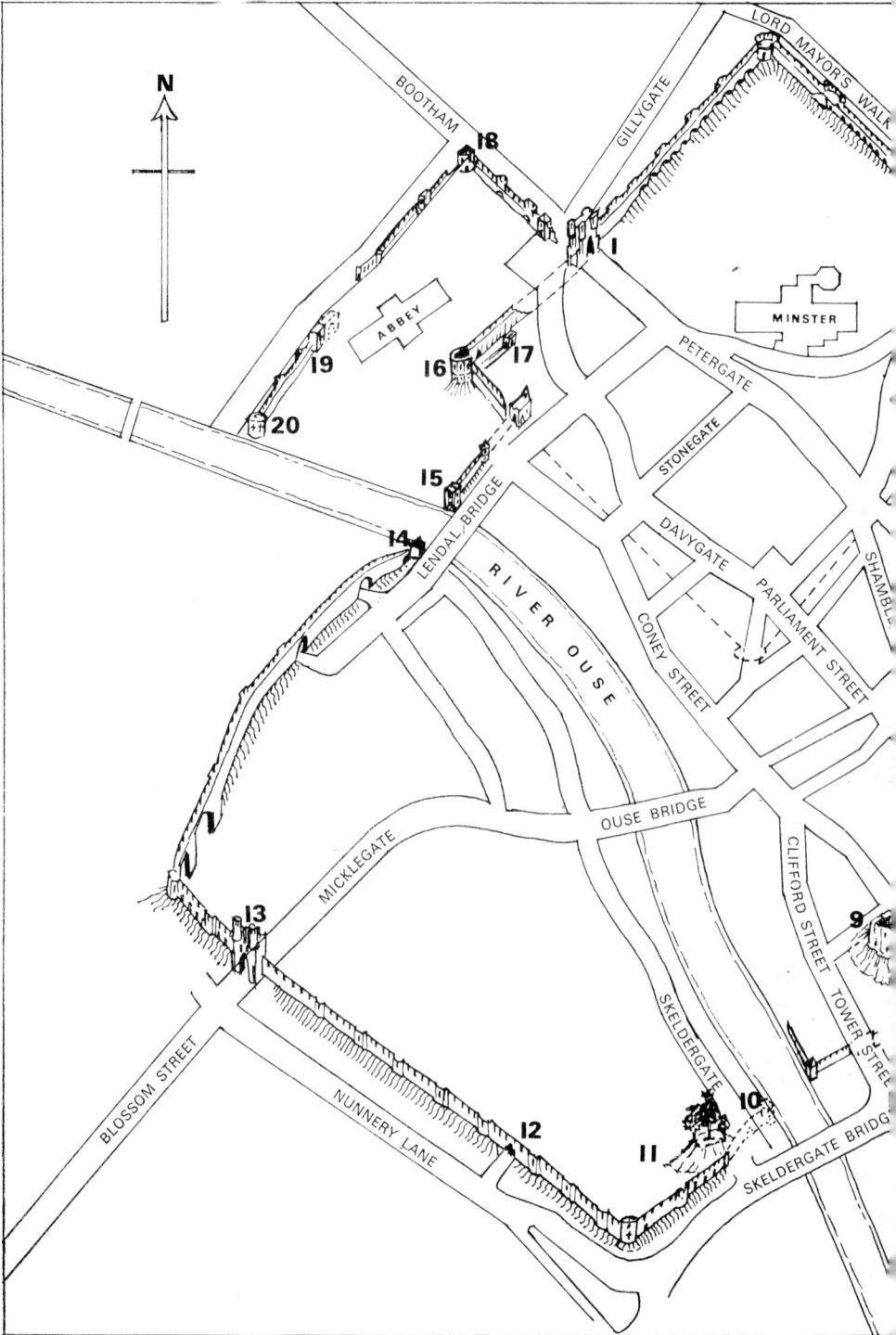

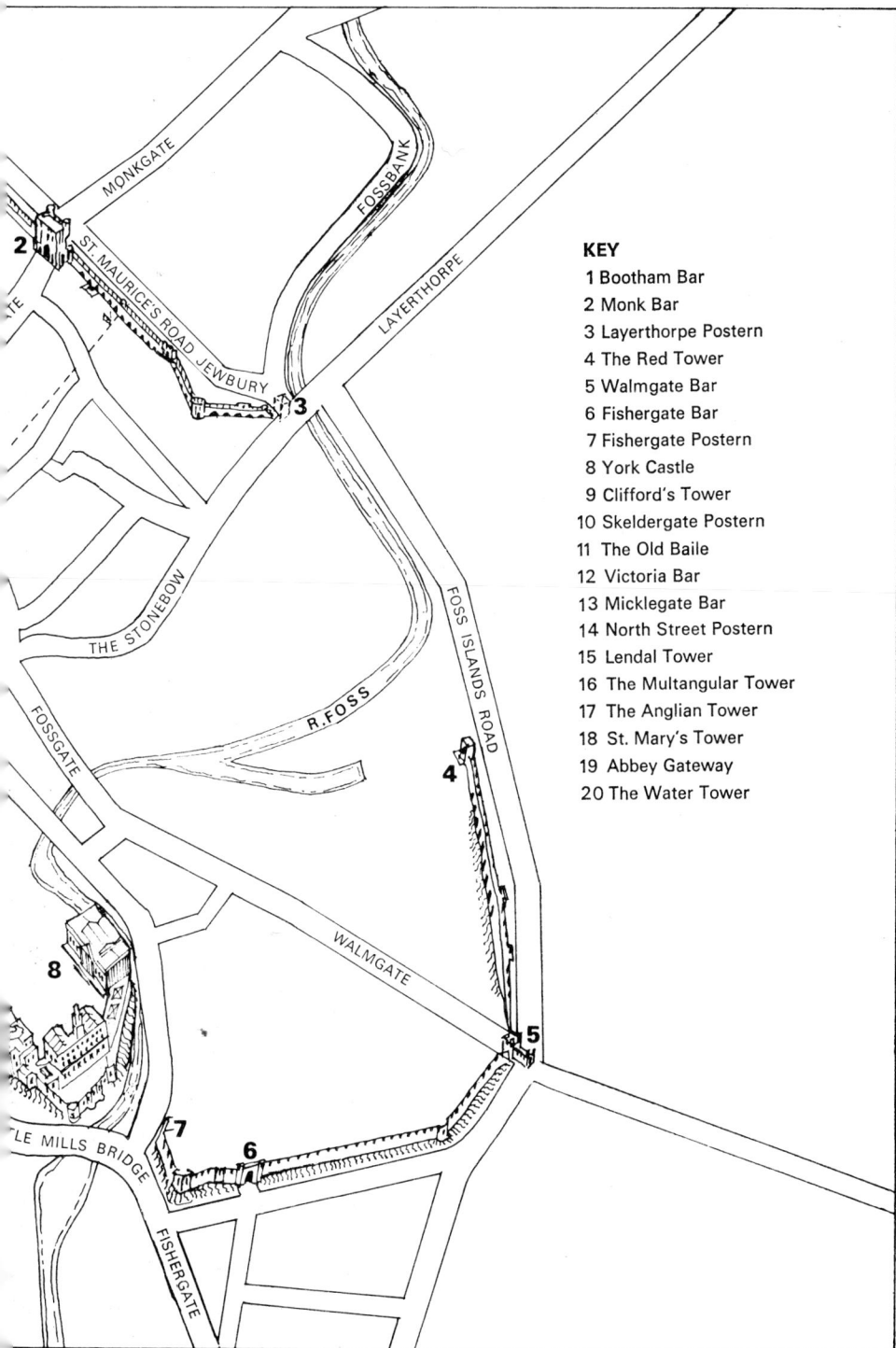

KEY

1. Bootham Bar
2. Monk Bar
3. Layerthorpe Postern
4. The Red Tower
5. Walmgate Bar
6. Fishergate Bar
7. Fishergate Postern
8. York Castle
9. Clifford's Tower
10. Skeldergate Postern
11. The Old Baile
12. Victoria Bar
13. Micklegate Bar
14. North Street Postern
15. Lendal Tower
16. The Multangular Tower
17. The Anglian Tower
18. St. Mary's Tower
19. Abbey Gateway
20. The Water Tower

although the ditch has been filled up and internally the earthwork has been cut back and revetted beside the deep cutting for the old station. Of the five towers which formerly existed one has been rebuilt beside the north railway arch, one has been destroyed for the farther road arch, and the others, two of them demi-hexagonal in plan, are still in good condition, although in only one are the inner rooms and embrasures for the arrow slits still accessible.

North Street Postern beside the Ouse was originally only a small square-headed doorway, even after enlargement to admit the Earl of Huntingdon's 'great horse' in 1577, but the present wide arch and two side passages were built by the Great North of England Railway Company in 1840 for access to their coal wharves. The £500 paid for permission to breach the walls was used by the Corporation to restore Walmgate Bar.

North Street Postern Tower   Crown Copyright

North Street Postern Tower, also called Barker Tower from the tanners' quarter near it, still retains its old arched embrasures, although the arrow-slits have been enlarged. An upper room with a conical tiled roof replaced the original flat roof in the seventeenth century, but the battlements are still preserved with windows formed in the embrasures. This tower was for centuries leased to the man operating a ferry across the Ouse; after the building of the bridge it became a mortuary and later a Parks Department store. It has recently been restored, exposing original features.

LENDAL TOWER TO BOOTHAM BAR

Lendal Tower, named from St. Leonard's Landing below the great medieval hospital, originally looked like a larger version of the tower opposite, but with a little turret on the north-west for a spiral staircase. An iron chain, noted by John Leland in about 1540, could be stretched to Barker Tower in order to close the river and prevent boatmen from

Lendal Tower   Crown Copyright

21

avoiding the payment of toll. The medieval tower was altered in the seventeenth century, when in 1616 it was first used as the base for an undertaking to supply the city with water. This was unsuccessful and the heightened tower remained derelict until 1677, when a similar enterprise was started. The building was enlarged and raised to four storeys with water from the river being pumped to a cistern on the roof and then circulated throughout York by means of wooden pipes.

At first a water-wheel operated the pump, then horse power, and finally a steam engine was installed in about 1760, rebuilt in 1784 by John Smeaton. This ran efficiently, supplying hot and cold water to adjoining baths until it was removed in 1836. The tower was lowered and restored with its present windows and battlements: it now serves as offices for the waterworks company, with a boardroom panelled in Jacobean style where once the massive beam engine worked. Of the medieval structure only the lower storey with two embrasures remains.

The city wall and rampart is now only preserved for a short stretch north-east of the tower beside the old cobbled street of Lendal Hill, and there has for long been a gap in the defences at the entrance to the Museum Gardens (the old grounds of St. Mary's Abbey) with their Gothic Lodge of 1874. By the arched water gate of St. Leonard's Hospital the city wall joined the Roman fortress wall, which has been exposed as far as the west angle and used as a base for the medieval wall, although until the thirteenth century it was presumably hidden under a post-Roman rampart.

The Multangular Tower was called Elrondyng in the fourteenth century but received its present name from Dr. Martin Lister, who first recognised its Roman origin in 1683. It is the west angle tower of the legionary fortress and was built in about 300 A.D. The small regular limestone facing blocks with a bonding course of red tiles, the work of Roman masons, can be distinguished between later patching at the base and the medieval wall with its arrow-slits above. The interior of the tower was cleared of earth in 1831 to reveal well-preserved Roman walling, but previously the ground surface was just below the ledge from which rise the arched embrasures around the cruciform slits. In the Middle Ages there was probably an embattled parapet around a flat or conical roof, since a stone spout still remains to drain off water, but the Roman building was even higher.

From the Multangular Tower to St. Leonard's Place the medieval wall stands on the Danish and Norman earth rampart, but in recent years this bank has been partly removed to reveal the buried Roman fortress wall. There is a narrow passage between the cobbled surface concealing underpinning of the city wall and the outer face of the uppermost 6 ft. (1·8 m) of the Roman wall, which in places retains the tile cornice above which stood the destroyed parapet. Some 10 ft. (3 m) from the rough inner side of the fortress wall is a fourteenth-century wall built by the authorities of St. Leonard's Hospital to retain the cut-back rampart. Part of a somewhat earlier building dug into the rampart can also be seen. Beyond the stumps of the side walls of a Roman internal interval tower is a unique building, only recently fully exposed to view.

The 'Anglian' Tower is square with two narrow arched side doorways and was vaulted in stone. Its masonry is of oolitic limestone from the Howardian Hills, not of the magnesian limestone from the Tadcaster area commonly used in the Roman and medieval buildings of York. It was built in a breach through the already ruined Roman wall, probably between 600 and 700. The fallen Roman battlements were replaced beside the tower by a timber parapet supported on a rubble revetment. Later both the tower and the Roman wall were buried under a broad earth mound, probably first heaped up by the Danish conquerors of York after 870. On this mound, enlarged after the Norman Conquest, the city walls were erected in about 1260. The buried tower was only re-discovered in 1839, when a tunnel was pierced through the ramparts to connect a stable within the walls to a garden outside them. It was excavated in 1969 by Jeffrey Radley, but in 1970 he was tragically killed by a fall of earth in a further trench cut to examine the defences outside the medieval walls. The cobbled revetment beyond the tower is stepped to indicate the outline of successive ramparts.

Between this point and Bootham Bar there is a wide breach in the walls made in 1831-35 when St. Leonard's Place was formed, destroying a tower. A hoard of several thousand Northumbrian coins discovered soon afterwards outside the De Grey Rooms must have been buried for safety in the internal rampart when the Vikings were attacking York in 867. A short length of Roman wall still stands beside the street.

THE WALLS OF ST. MARY'S ABBEY

The walls of St. Mary's Abbey joined the city's defences at Bootham Bar. The abbey had been founded in about 1080 in the shelter of an old fortification which had been the seat of the Saxon Earls of Northumbria and so was known as Earlsborough. It became one of the richest and most important Benedictine monasteries in England, but was frequently at odds with the citizens of York. Its protective walls were built in 1266 and heightened by about 6 ft. (1.8 m) in 1318, when battlements and new towers were added. The rectangular tower and postern near the Bar in Exhibition Square were, however, built in 1497 as a rear entrance to the Abbot's House, which became the King's Manor, a royal palace and the seat from 1540 to 1641 of the Council of the North. The small side passage was made in 1836. The tower, constructed of brick behind a stone facing, has two well-preserved cruciform gun-loops, visible internally but concealed on the outside by the adjoining building. The abbey walls are generally well-preserved and have been revealed in this century by the gradual demolition of houses built against them since 1645. Beside Bootham can be seen two semi-circular towers rising above the narrow wall-walk, the first retaining the stump of a pinnacle on one battlement. Many masons' marks are cut into the stones of this length of wall.

St. Mary's Tower stands at the corner of Bootham and Marygate. This round tower was built in about 1325. After the dissolution of the abbey in 1539 it was used to store the records of many Yorkshire monasteries, but at noon on 16th June 1644 a mine was exploded under it by the besieging forces commanded by the Earl of Manchester. The outer half collapsed, killing some defenders and destroying the documents, although some were salvaged from the ruins by Roger Dodsworth

St. Mary's Tower   Crown Copyright

and still survive in York Minster Library. The tower was rebuilt in something like its old form with materials from a ruined wing of the Manor, including window mullions and an arcaded frieze, but the join is still clearly visible between the old and new walling.

Along Marygate can be seen in many merlons the slots for wooden shutters to close the embrasures and there is still a rectangular tower once containing a small doorway. Adjoining the churchyard of St. Olave's are remains of a long building, perhaps the almonry, with slit windows and a doorway at the south end, formerly protected with a portcullis. The church itself was rebuilt in the eighteenth century in a medieval style. Beyond it are remains of St. Mary's Chapel and of the principal gateway to the abbey with its Norman outer arch and the arcaded side walls of the passage. This gatehouse remained intact until about 1700 and its upper part was of one build with the surviving St. Mary's Lodge of about 1460.

The whole range housed a court room for the Liberty of St. Mary's on the upper floor.

St. Mary's Water Tower   Crown Copyright

Beyond the remains of the gatehouse the precinct wall is lower and the two rounded towers are small ones. There is a nineteenth-century arch to the riverside walk and the wall now ends at another round tower (the

25

Water Tower) which retains its arrow-slits and doorway but has lost its crenellated parapet since 1700. There was once a wall along the river front of the abbey grounds, later known as the Manor Shore, but this has long since been destroyed, as has most of the abbey boundary wall along the outer edge of the city ditch, although a short length can be seen adjoining the car park at the Exhibition Square end of the lane between the King's Manor and the city walls.

THE HISTORY OF THE DEFENCES
The first fortifications

The centre of York is on the site of the Roman *Eburacum*, founded in 71 A.D. as the base of the Ninth Legion, replaced in about 125 by the Sixth Legion. The Roman settlement consisted of a fortress, 50 acres in extent (123 ha.), on the north-east bank of the Ouse with suburbs to the south and west, and of a civil town or *colonia* on the opposite bank. The fortress defences in their final state as rebuilt by the emperor Constantius I in about 300 A.D. were a wall 5 ft. thick (1·5 m.), and about 20 ft. high (6 m.), backed by an internal rampart, and an outer ditch. There were four gateways, under the present St. Helen's Square, Bootham Bar, the rampart north-west of Monk Bar, and King's Square respectively. The lines of the principal internal streets between these gateways are still followed by Stonegate, Petergate, and Chapter House Street. On the south-west or river front of the fortress there were large projecting polygonal towers, one at each angle, and six smaller towers at regular intervals between them. The towers along the rest of the circuit were rectangular and internal. The *colonia*, linked to the fortress by a bridge opposite the present Guildhall, and with its main streets represented by Tanner Row and the upper end of Micklegate, also had walls of which little is known.

Under the Anglian kings of Northumbria the Roman fortress walls seem to have remained the main defence of the royal capital with its cathedral founded in 627 in or near the partly-ruined headquarters building under the present Minster. One breach in the walls was filled by a stone-built vaulted tower and another gap at the east angle was blocked with a palisade. A timber breastwork supported on a rough stone revetment was made to replace the Roman battlements, but later, after the Danish capture of the city in 867, the ancient wall was buried along three sides under an earth bank, no doubt crowned with a stockade. This bank extended south-eastwards towards landing stages on the marshy banks of the Foss, which then flowed more to the west than nowadays, protecting a post-Roman extension of the city. A similar rampart burying the Roman wall around the civil town was probably thrown up to defend the merchants' settlement on the south-west bank of the Ouse.

Changes made by the Normans

After the Norman Conquest the existing defences were heightened and extended on the north-east to include St. Cuthbert's Church. A suburb straggling along Walmgate on the east side of the Foss was probably also enclosed by a rampart at this time. In 1068 and 1069 William the Conqueror built two castles, one on each bank of the Ouse at the south-east end of the city. Houses were ruthlessly cleared away for these twin fortresses, affecting a whole shire or ward of York. When these castles were soon afterwards destroyed by English rebels he rebuilt them after devastating the disaffected northern counties. Both had a motte or mound to support a wooden tower and a bailey or courtyard below. Of these two fortifications that on the north-east bank remained a centre of royal power and was known as York Castle. The other, the Old Baile, soon fell into disuse as a fortress. King William also dammed the river Foss just below the more important castle, flooding meadows and orchards to form the extensive King's Fishpond. The Castle Mills beside the dam remained until the nineteenth century.

During the 12th Century

The gateways through the ramparts were rebuilt in stone and arches of this date still exist at Bootham, Micklegate and Walmgate Bars. Another archway which once stood where Victoria Bar was later built was called Lounlith, the hidden gate, in contrast to Micklelith, the great gate. Bootham Bar, which takes its present name from the suburb of booths outside the defences, was earlier called Galmanlith, after the slope of Galmhou where St. Mary's Abbey was founded.

Strengthening of the Defences

In 1190, one of the castles, probably the principal one, was burned down by rioters attacking the York Jews who had taken refuge there. In 1215 Geoffrey de Neville, King John's Chamberlain and Sheriff of Yorkshire, strengthened the fortifications. His widening of the ditch destroyed houses built beside it and damaged the castle mills. In 1228 the wooden tower of the rebuilt castle was blown down by gales and when King Henry III visited York in 1244 he resolved to rebuild the castle in stone. As a result, the keep on the motte, now called Clifford's Tower, the bailey walls with two twin-towered gateways and six or seven other towers, and prisons, halls, a chapel and a kitchen within the castle, were erected between 1245 and 1260.

Henry III also stimulated the citizens to replace their ancient palisade with a stone wall by granting them the right to collect murage, a tax on goods brought into the city, to be used for the building and repair of the defences. Between 1250 and 1270 the curtain walls were built around the older parts of York, extending from the boundary of the Old Baile near Victoria Bar to the Ouse at North Street and from St. Leonard's Landing opposite to the Foss at Layerthorpe. At first there were probably only a few interval towers—those of a D-shaped or semi-circular plan seen to be the oldest—and the upper parts of the Bars were also added later. In 1266 St. Mary's Abbey surrounded its precinct on the landward side with a similar stone wall, and in 1285 permission was given to fortify the Minster Close.

Defensive measures during the Scottish Wars

The danger from Scottish raids, which in 1319 and 1327 extended close to York, led the citizens to add barbicans in front of the gateways, portcullises within them and upper storeys with turrets. From 1318 onwards St. Mary's Abbey heightened its precinct wall, added towers and fortified the river front. In 1345 the building of a stone curtain wall around the Walmgate suburb was commenced. From that year there survives a contract made between the mayor and citizens and Master Thomas de Staunton, a mason, for the erection of the length between Fishergate Bar and the Foss opposite the Castle. The document lays down the required thickness and height as well as the rate of payment; Master Thomas, who gave as a guarantor Lord Henry Percy, was given an option on carrying out further work on the Walmgate defences. Apart from this contract and lists, made in 1316, 1380, and 1403, of the parishes and constables responsible for the maintenance and guarding of specified lengths of wall, the records which throw most light on the building of the medieval defences are the regular grants of murage in the Patent Rolls and the occasional reference in other royal archives. The House Books, or minutes of York City Council, and the Chamberlains' Accounts are preserved in a continuous series only from the late fifteenth century.

During the Fifteenth and Sixteenth Centuries

York Castle, which had housed the royal courts and treasury during the Scottish wars of Edward I, II and III, was neglected as a fortress and royal residence during the fifteenth century, although the gaol and mint there was still maintained. Henry VII was anxious that the defences of York, a city notable for loyalty to Richard III, should be strengthened against further rebellions. As a result new towers (the Red Tower and Fishergate Postern Tower) were built at either end of the Walmgate defences, a wall-walk carried on arcades was added along part of the circuit, and a length of wall was restored near Fishergate Bar. However, that gateway and Walmgate Bar were burned by rebels in 1489 and the former was so badly damaged that it remained walled up

28

for three centuries. The king also wanted cannon to be supplied for each gate—the city had possessed some guns as early as 1463—but these were not obtained until 1511. In spite of these precautions the Pilgrims of Grace, led by Robert Aske, captured York in 1535. The antiquary John Leland visited the city soon afterwards and has left the first description of the walls, noting the number of towers and the ruinous condition of the Castle. The defences were again strengthened in 1569, when a revolt led by the Earls of Northumberland and Westmorland threatened York. Later in Elizabeth I's reign new timber-framed houses were built over three Bars; that at Walmgate still remains.

The Defences during Siege and the Civil War

At the outbreak of the Civil War in 1642 York was garrisoned for King Charles I by the Earl of Cumberland and then by William Cavendish, Earl (and later Duke) of Newcastle. Clifford's Tower was repaired to house the main garrison and arsenal, while earthwork forts were constructed on the ridge to the south of the city. From 23rd April, 1644, Newcastle's army was besieged in York by the Scottish army under the Earl of Leven, quartered to the south, and by the Parliamentarians of Yorkshire commanded by Lord Fairfax, who took up positions to the east. These combined forces were not large enough to surround the whole perimeter and blockade the city completely until the arrival six weeks later of the army of the Eastern Counties led by the Earl of Manchester. Their arrival brought the total number of besiegers to about 30,000.

The course of the siege from day to day can be followed with the aid of diaries and newsletters written by those within the encircled city or by chaplains with the Parliamentary forces, and there is even a Latin epic poem on the siege written by one soldier. On 5th June, the besiegers established a five-gun battery on Lamel Hill east of York, now in the grounds of The Retreat Hospital. During the following night they captured two of the three forts to the south, although the central earthwork which straddled the road from Tadcaster and from which the Mount derives its name, continued to hold out. The Royalists then set fire to the suburbs in Bootham, Gillygate, Monkgate, and Lawrence Street to prevent the houses being used as cover by the enemy. Newcastle, who had enforced rationing within the walls, learned from messengers who had passed through the enemy lines disguised as women that the king had ordered Prince Rupert to relieve York. He therefore opened negotiations with the Parliamentary generals in order to gain time.

On 16th June, the besiegers exploded a mine under St. Mary's Tower on the Abbey walls, but a party which penetrated to the King's Manor was soon cut off and its members captured or killed. The Parliamentarians were disheartened by this failure and their lack of pay and ammunition caused talk of mutiny. Prince Rupert's army, advancing from Lancashire, relieved York on 1st July, and the besieging forces started to retreat towards Tadcaster. During the next evening, however, the combined armies of Prince Rupert and Newcastle were disastrously defeated at Marston Moor 6 miles (10 km.) west of York and the victors were able to resume the siege. Sir James Glemham, now the Governor, surrendered the city on favourable terms, and on 16th July it was occupied by a Parliamentary garrison. Lord Fairfax protected the Minster and churches from damage after the surrender.

The walls had been damaged by the bombardment and repairs were needed, especially to Bootham and Walmgate Bars. Parliament assigned £5,000 for this purpose from the confiscated estates of Royalists. New gun platforms and guard houses were built at various points and by 1648 most of the damage was repaired. Clifford's Tower remained a garrison with one or more companies of infantry until 1684 when it was accidentally gutted by an explosion in the store of powder. Many details are known of the condition of the defences during the late seventeenth century, both from artists such as Francis Place, from surveyors like James Archer who drew a map of the city in about 1675, and from writers including Sir John Reresby, who was the royal Governor of York until supporters of William III seized control of the city in 1688.

The changed conditions of the Eighteenth Century

Although the defences were in good repair the crisis of 1745 revealed how inadequate were the medieval walls to meet attack by contemporary weapons. It was feared that Prince Charles Edward's Jacobite army might cross the Pennines during its advance from Scotland and attack York. Precautions taken included the deepening of the surrounding ditches, the lowering of the ramparts so that the walls were everywhere at least 10 ft. high (3 m.), and the repair of gates and portcullises. Four volunteer companies of infantry were recruited in the city, and fox-hunting gentlemen of the district formed a light cavalry force—the Royal Regiment of Hunters, with Major-General Oglethorpe, the former colonist of Georgia as its colonel. The danger from the Jacobites soon passed with their defeat at Culloden, and the walls were allowed to become pleasure walks or were pierced beside the Bars with new openings for pedestrians.

The Castle lost its appearance of a medieval fortress with the demolition of a gatehouse and towers, and with the building of a palatial prison, courthouse, and female gaol. Bootham Bar had received a new inner front built in classical style with a statue of Ebrauk, the city's

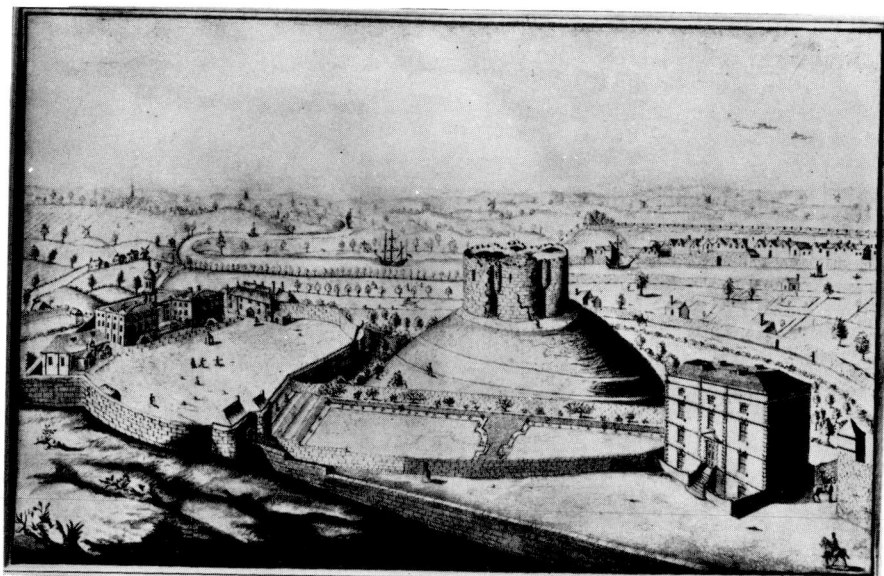

York Castle, early 18th century

mythical founder. Lendal Tower, which housed the steam pump supplying York with water from the Ouse, was heightened. The Red Tower fell into ruin.

The beginning of Preservation Work

By the end of the eighteenth century the need to retain the city walls was seriously doubted and in 1799 the corporation resolved to destroy them. As a first step Skeldergate Postern was pulled down in 1807, but the Archbishop sued the city for damages on the grounds of loss of tolls collected there and at other gates during the Lammastide fair. The success of this lawsuit made the city more cautious, and when the Archbishop, Dean and Chapter applied to the Exchequer Court for an injunction to restrain the council from demolishing the walls the threatened destruction was further deterred. Meanwhile an alliance of antiquaries and those who valued the right of walking along the wall, including the artist William Etty, pressed for the restoration and preservation of the defences. Private subscriptions enabled a committee to restore the walls from Skeldergate to North Street. The controversy caused several artists to record the appearance of the Bars, towers, and curtain walls in face of the danger that they would vanish for ever.

31

Layerthorpe Postern in about 1770

This period of grave peril to the walls lasted until about 1860, but in the end losses were confined to Castlegate Postern, removed for extensions to the Castle prison, Layerthorpe postern, the barbicans in front of Monk Bar, Micklegate Bar, and Bootham Bar, and a stretch of wall and rampart to make St. Leonard's Place. Victoria Bar was made in 1838, archways for the railway lines to the old station in Tanner Row were pierced in 1839 and 1845, and the narrow North Street Postern was replaced by a triple opening in 1840. Walmgate Bar was restored in the same year. When in 1855 the Board of Health Committee recommended the removal of much of the walls around the Walmgate area the proposal was heavily defeated. The whole circuit of the walls was eventually restored, ending in 1889 with the length from Bootham Bar to Monk Bar. Arches pierced in 1874 for access to the present railway station outside the walls did little damage. By then York had become more prosperous as a centre for the new form of transport and suburbs in the former fields and meadows outside the old limits had drastically changed its appearance.

The site of St. Mary's Abbey was obtained by the Yorkshire Philosophical Society, founded in 1822, and there the Museum Gardens were laid out with the Multangular Tower excavated and displayed. The new Yorkshire Museum became a centre for increased antiquarian interest in York and its past. The Abbey precinct wall was gradually exposed to view by the demolition of most of the houses built against it since the seventeenth century.

Historic Monuments

The city has restored the walls, gateways and towers. The ramparts have been planted with spring flowers, the wall-walks made safe, and later alterations removed. In 1935 York acquired most of its ancient Castle, disused as a prison since 1929, and has been able to open in the eighteenth-century buildings one of the most popular and attractive museums in the country. The defences, scheduled as ancient monuments in 1922, and listed as historic buildings under the Town and Country Planning Acts, are carefully maintained and more appreciated. Together with the Minster and the old parish churches and guildhalls they are a vivid link with York's medieval past.

FURTHER NOTES ON THE DEFENCES

Payment for building the Walls originally came from the murage tax levied on imports and contracts like that of 1345 would be made with masons to design and erect them. During the fifteenth century it seems that payment for repair came from money especially set aside from murage receipts or from rents of gateways and towers leased as houses or storerooms, of ramparts let for their grass as hay, or of moats profitable for fishing. Later, however, the cost of maintenance was borne by the general income of the city. During the period 1459-1520 the city employed a Common Mason whose principal task was to direct the repair of the walls and bridges. From 1489 until 1577 muremasters, usually four in number, were elected annually from among the citizens. Their job was to ensure the repair of the walls (*muri* in Latin), and then to recover their expenditure from the chamberlains. This was a burdensome and unpopular office and so was made a necessary preliminary to election to the more honourable positions of chamberlain, sheriff, and mayor. The task was eventually given to a salaried official, the Common Husband, later renamed Corporation Surveyor, and finally merged with the post of City Engineer.

From the city records it is often still possible to trace the whole course of work on a gateway or length of wall. A complaint would be made in a Wardmote—the gathering of citizens in one of the four wards—and then raised in the City Council. A committee might be appointed to inspect the defect, would report back, and then the Council would resolve on work and eventually authorise payment. The expenditure would finally be recorded in the Chamberlains' rolls and Books of Account. Some of the original bills and receipts may even survive. In modern times the reports of the Estates Committee and of the City Treasurer will provide similar evidence. It is in the Chamberlains' accounts of about 1685 that the term Bar Walls by which they are generally described in York newspapers first occurs, but it then meant the walls near one of the four main Bars: e.g. by Micklegate Bar Walls was intended the city walls in Micklegate Ward.

Manning in Wartime

During the period known in most detail—from 1500 onwards—York's defences were only seldom overhauled and manned to meet an expected attack or siege. Precautions taken in 1569, 1642-4, and 1745 are known: the posterns were blocked with earth and stones, ladders and combustible material were brought in from the suburbs, boats on the rivers were secured and outer earthworks thrown up. The narrow ledges which survive unaltered in a few places—behind the Central Library, from Tower Street to the Ouse, and along St. Mary's Abbey walls—show that the medieval walls were not normally patrolled and records made during times of crisis indicate that when danger threatened planks were used to provide a wider parapet walk for archers. The provision by various parishes of constables and their responsibility for the repair of lengths of wall, recorded during the fourteenth century, had lapsed by the reign of Elizabeth I, but by then there were arrangements for the recruitment and training in times of peril of bowmen, musketeers and pikemen.

From 1642 onwards the city had a garrison of soldiers and a royal or parliamentary governor. Some of this force guarded Clifford's Tower, while others were stationed at the gateways. It was not until 1688, shortly before his capture by the rebels against James II, that the Governor, Sir John Reresby, handed over the keys of the city to the Lord Mayor. Cannon had been mounted on the Bars as early as 1511, although York had possessed some guns during the Wars of the Roses, and their numbers were increased to about thirty in 1642, with larger batteries on top of Clifford's Tower, on the roof of St. Olave's Church and on Baile Hill, but most were removed to Hull after the war. A few still remained at the Tower until 1690 together with a store of gunpowder. It seems that regular soldiers last guarded the gates in 1757, when there were riots against a tax to support the militia, but from 1795 York has been a permanent military station with barracks for infantry and, until recently, for cavalry.

Watchmen

In normal times there were only one or two watchmen at each Bar and postern who locked the gates at nightfall and opened them at dawn—in summer they were usually closed from 9 p.m. to 4 a.m. If citizens urgently needed to get in or out of York they were expected to tip the watchmen for their trouble. Occasionally impatient people might borrow or even copy the keys or a surly guardian refuse entrance; such occurrences appear in the records when the culprits came before the city courts.

Royal visits, assizes, epidemics of plague, and the stricter insistence on the observance of Lent or of the Sabbath led to regulations increasing the number of watchmen. Details of the ceremonial reception of kings, usually at Micklegate Bar, were set down in the House Books as precedents for future occasions, so that the words of the pageants enacted before Henry VII or of the fulsome speech made to James I can still be read. James I and Charles I were greeted with pageantry at Micklegate Bar, but in times of plague the gates were watched to prevent the entry of visitors and goods coming from infected areas. When plague was reported at nearby towns the entry of travellers and of merchandise was strictly controlled. In the autumn of 1603 a citizen was imprisoned for helping a merchant to climb over the walls near Monk Bar with his pack, as was the watchman at Walmgate Bar who told an apprentice loaded with sugar and spice to come back at night and he would get these goods over the walls. During Lent representatives of the butchers' and fishmongers' guilds shared the watch to prevent fresh meat being imported. On Sundays in the seventeenth century citizens were prevented by the gatekeepers from leaving York for country alehouses instead of hearing sermons in church.

Special use of Bars

A regulation was made in 1501 for knockers to be attached to the city gates to be used by any Scot wishing to enter York on pain of imprisonment. Among earlier measures to be taken in wartime had been the ejection from the city of all Scots and rascals. Although it is not

Monk Bar in about 1820

certain that such knockers were ever put up, stocks and whipping posts by the Bars and ducking stools near the posterns were certainly used and the gateways were thought to be appropriate places for displaying the heads of traitors—in Shakespeare's *Henry VI* Queen Margaret orders the head of Richard Duke of York to be set on York gate 'that York may overlook the town of York' — and the practice continued to 1752. Later they were plastered with advertisements for coaches or medicines. Now the only plaques they bear record their history and restoration, while the figures above them are of stone not flesh.